CLAIRE LAMSDALE

Who is
Henry Kazwell?

CORNELSEN
ENGLISH
LIBRARY

Cornelsen

CORNELSEN **ENGLISH** LIBRARY

Claire Lamsdale, Susan Abbey, Frank Donoghue · Who is Henry Kazwell?

Verlagsredaktion
Mara Leibowitz

Umschlaggestaltung
hawemannundmosch, Konzeption und Gestaltung, Berlin

Titelbild
Sunrise over the English Channel [M]: mauritius images/Alamy/
Malcolm Fairman

Illustration
www.davidnorman.com, Meerbusch

Gestaltung & technische Umsetzung
Annika Preyhs für Buchgestaltung+, Berlin

Passende Arbeitsblätter und weitere Hilfen zu diesem Titel gibt es unter:
www.cornelsen.de/cel

www.cornelsen.de

1. Auflage, 6. Druck 2024

Alle Drucke dieser Auflage sind inhaltlich unverändert und können
im Unterricht nebeneinander verwendet werden.

© 2013 Cornelsen Schulverlage GmbH, Berlin
© 2018 Cornelsen Verlag GmbH, Berlin

Druck: H. Heenemann, Berlin

ISBN 978-3-06-033219-9

PEFC zertifiziert
Dieses Produkt stammt aus nachhaltig
bewirtschafteten Wäldern und kontrollierten
Quellen.

www.pefc.de

PEFC/04-31-1156

CONTENTS

CHAPTER 1 **People call me Kaz**

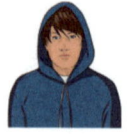

Kaz opened the big gate and looked up and down the street. It was quiet, so he pushed his bike through it. The gate closed behind him with a 'click'.

It was a nice Monday morning in Plymouth – sunny and warm. Kaz got on the bike and he went along Hoe Road.

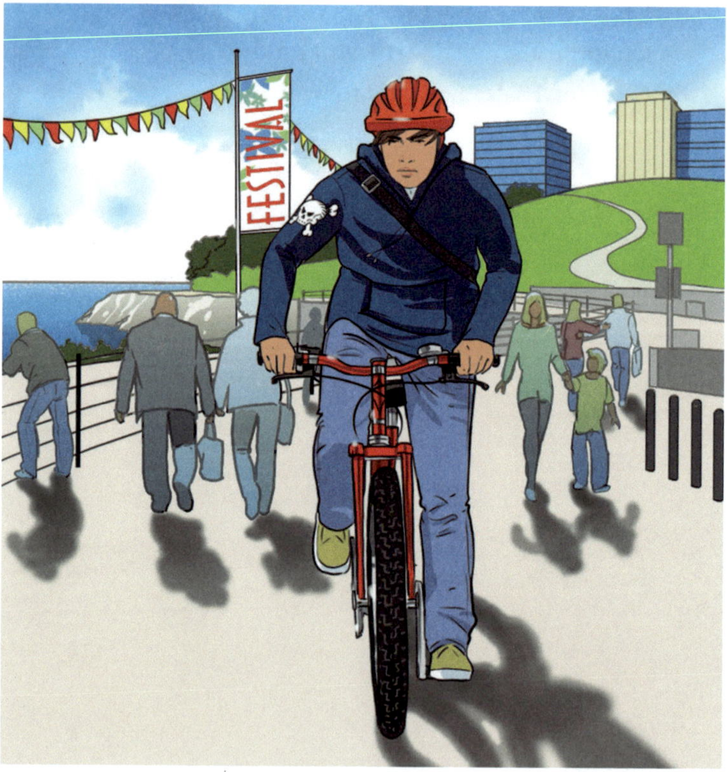

The town was busy. It was summer, and there were lots of tourists in Plymouth. It was the Plymouth Summer Festival too, so there were visitors in town for that.

Kaz liked Plymouth. It was different from his hometown – London. It wasn't so big and there wasn't so much traffic. So he could ride his bike everywhere. Of course there was the sea in Plymouth too – the beautiful sea. Kaz was happy that he wasn't in London now. London was the past and he didn't want to think about the past. Plymouth was the future for Kaz.

'Good morning, Henry!' Tom Jones shouted when he saw the boy on the bike. The old man was outside his small shop on Radford Street.

'It's Kaz, Mr Jones. My name is Henry Kazwell, but people call me Kaz,' the boy answered.

'OK, Kaz. Well, I'm Tom – not Mr Jones,' the old man said and laughed.

'OK, Tom,' Kaz answered.

'Now Kaz, can you help me with these boxes of apples, please? I'm too old for this hard work,' Tom said.

'No problem,' Kaz answered. He put his bike next to the shop and he locked it carefully.

Then Kaz saw another boy. He was younger – about 13. He was outside a cafe, near Tom's shop. The boy saw Kaz too. He looked at Kaz's bike. Then the boy said, 'Hello. Nice bike.' But Kaz looked away. He didn't want to talk to the boy. What did this boy want? Why was he interested in Kaz's bike? Did he know this bike?

Kaz went into the shop and he started his new job. There was lots of work. First he washed the floor. Then he filled the shelves with lots of things like bread, biscuits, cakes and tins of beans. After that he put fruit outside the shop – apples, bananas, oranges. He saw the boy at the cafe again. They didn't speak and Kaz went back into the shop quickly.

Kaz worked hard all morning. Tom was very happy with his new helper. He was a quiet boy; he didn't talk a lot.

'Take a break, Kaz,' Tom said. 'You're working very hard.'

But Kaz didn't stop. Lots of customers came in and Kaz helped them. He took bags and boxes to their cars. He saw the other boy again, but he was very busy too, because there were lots of people in the cafe.

Kaz had a big bag of potatoes in his hands. It fell on his foot and he shouted, 'Oh, blimey!'

Tom laughed. 'Are you OK?' he asked the boy.

'Yeah, I'm fine, thanks,' Kaz answered.

'You must be from London with an accent like that,' Tom said.

'Yes,' Kaz answered. 'I'm from London. I live here now.'

'Are your parents here?' Tom asked.

'Er … just my dad … he's a sailor …' Kaz answered.

'That's very interesting,' Tom said. 'I was a sailor too, when I was younger.'

Kaz picked up the bag and started to work again. He didn't want to talk about his dad.

What happened in the last chapter? Kaz is new in Plymouth. He moved here from London and he has started a job at Tom Jones' shop. He saw a boy in the street. The boy said 'hello', but Kaz was very quiet and didn't want to talk to him.

5 Adam Osmanovic opened the cafe door. He looked up. It was a nice morning – sunny and warm. It was the summer holidays and Adam had no school – that was great! But he had to work with his mum in her cafe. That wasn't so great!

10 Adam looked at a poster in the cafe window:

'I'd love to go to the funfair,' he thought. But the cafe was always busy in the summer and it was very, very busy when the Summer Festival was here. So Adam had to help his mum.

Plymouth Summer Festival

Monday, 20th July:
* Funfair on the Hoe – all day
* Big fireworks show 9 pm
All are welcome!

Then Adam saw old Tom Jones outside his shop.
15 'Good morning, Tom,' he shouted.
'Hello Adam,' the old man answered. 'No school today?'
'No – we have holidays now,' Adam answered.
'Lucky you! I'd like a holiday too,' Tom laughed. 'But I have to work.'
20 'I have to work too,' Adam said and smiled.

Adam saw a boy on a nice red bike. It was a mountain bike – a very expensive mountain bike. The boy stopped at Tom's shop. He had a nice blue jacket too – a designer jacket.

5   'A rich kid!' Adam thought. 'What does he want here?'

Adam waited at the cafe door and watched. The boy was bigger than Adam. He was older too – maybe 15 or 16.

Tom came out of his shop with a big box of apples. He looked tired. But Tom looked happy to see the boy on the

red bike. Maybe he was Tom's grandson. The boy spoke with Tom but Adam couldn't hear what they said. Tom laughed. Adam was very interested. Then suddenly the boy looked at Adam. Adam waved and spoke to the boy,
5 but he didn't answer. He didn't smile. He just looked away.

'That's strange,' Adam thought. 'I'm sure he heard me. But maybe he's very shy.'

The boy put his red bike next to Tom's shop and he locked it. Then he went into the shop and he didn't look at
10 Adam again.

The first customers started to arrive at the cafe. Two people sat at a table outside.

'An English breakfast, please,' the man said to Adam.

'For me too, please,' the woman said.

15 Adam went inside and helped his mum to make the breakfasts. When he came out again, there were a lot more customers.

'This is going to be a busy day,' he thought.

Adam looked at Tom's shop again. The red bike was still
20 there. Then he saw the boy again. He had a box of fruit in his hands.

'What's he doing there at the shop?' Adam asked himself.

The boy looked at Adam and quickly looked away
25 again.

'That's really strange,' Adam thought. 'That boy is hiding something. Something isn't right. Tom always works alone.' Adam was a bit worried. He liked Tom and

9

he hoped everything was OK in Tom's shop. Why was that boy there? Who was he? Adam had to find out more.

Later that morning Adam's friends Mia, Luca and Ellie came to the cafe.

5   'Come on, Adam. Let's go to the funfair,' Mia said.

'I can't. I have to help Mum,' Adam answered.

'You can go to the fireworks this evening,' Adam's mum said. 'Now, back to work. The cafe is really busy.'

Adam told his friends about the boy with the red bike, 10 but they just laughed.

'Oh, Adam, you're too suspicious!' Luca said.

CHAPTER 3   **Kaz in the cafe**

What happened in the last chapter? Adam saw Kaz at Tom's shop and he was suspicious. Why was he there? Who was he? He didn't understand. The cafe was very busy and Adam 15 had to work hard.

Kaz had a very busy morning in Tom's shop. He didn't talk a lot, he just worked. He saw the boy at the cafe again. That boy just looked at him, but Kaz looked away. 'What does that boy 20 want?' he asked himself.

Tom liked his new helper. He was very quiet, but he worked hard. At one o'clock Tom said, 'OK, Kaz. Your morning is over. It's time to go home.'

'But I can stay longer, Tom,' Kaz answered.

'No thanks, you've helped me a lot. I only need you for the mornings,' the old man answered. 'Go to the funfair with your friends. Have a nice afternoon,' Tom said.

'I'm new here. I don't have any friends,' Kaz answered.

5 'Go and talk to Adam in the cafe. He's a nice boy and maybe you two can be friends,' Tom said.

Kaz didn't answer. He didn't really want to make new friends. He didn't want to talk to other people.

'Kaz, can you go to the cafe and buy a pasty for me, 10 please? Here's £3.50.'

Kaz took the money and walked to the cafe. There were lots of people there. He saw the boy and a woman. But they were very busy and they didn't see Kaz at first.

'A spaghetti Bolognese, please,' one woman said.

15 'Vegetable soup for me, please,' a man said.

The boy went from table to table. At last he saw Kaz.

'Hello,' he said. 'Can I help you?'

'Er … a pasty for Tom, please,' Kaz said.

Kaz waited. The boy got the pasty.

20 'That's £3.49, please,' he said. 'Do you work for Tom?'

'Yes,' Kaz answered. 'But only in the mornings.'

'Do you like the work?' the boy asked.

'Yes, it's OK,' Kaz answered. He didn't really want to chat. Kaz looked at all the people in the cafe. 'I could help 25 you here in the afternoons,' he said.

The woman heard this.

'Have you worked in a cafe before?' she asked.

'Yes, I helped in a cafe in London,' Kaz answered.

'What's your name?' the boy asked.

30 'Henry Kazwell – but people call me Kaz,' he answered.

'Hi Kaz. I'm Adam. And this is my mum,' the boy said.

'How old are you, Kaz?' Adam's mum asked.

'16,' Kaz said.

'OK, Kaz. Take the pasty to Tom. Then come back to the cafe and you can help me in the kitchen. It's very messy,' Adam's mum said.

So that afternoon Kaz worked in the kitchen of the cafe. He worked hard. When Adam came into the kitchen, he asked Kaz some questions.

'Where are you from?' Adam asked.

'London.' Kaz didn't say a lot.

A bit later Adam asked, 'What school do you go to?'

But Kaz didn't answer. Maybe he didn't hear the question.

5 Later, when it was quieter in the cafe, Adam's mum asked, 'Kaz, are you hungry? Do you want some food?'

Kaz was very hungry. First she gave him some spaghetti bolognese. He ate that, but he was still hungry. Then Adam's mum gave him some chips. And after that he had some cake. Adam's mum was surprised.

'Wow, you have a great appetite!' she said.

At about 5 o'clock some kids came to the cafe.

'These are my friends – Luca, Mia and Ellie,' Adam said. 'And this is Kaz.' The three friends smiled. Kaz said hi, and then he went into the back of the restaurant with some boxes.

'He looks nice,' Ellie whispered to Mia.

Mia smiled. She agreed with Ellie.

'OK, Adam. Your work is over. You can go to town now. Here's some money for ice cream for everybody,' Adam's mum said.

'Do you want to come too?' Ellie asked Kaz when he came back again.

'Oh, I don't know …' Kaz answered.

'Oh, come on. It'll be fun,' Mia said. So Kaz said OK. But he wasn't sure.

What happened in the last chapter? Kaz started a new afternoon job in the cafe. But he didn't talk a lot to Adam. So Adam is still suspicious. Then Kaz met Adam's friends. Mia and Ellie thought that he was nice!

5 Adam, Mia, Luca and Ellie were excited. Plymouth was a great place in the summer. And they loved the Summer Festival. Tonight was the 10 night of the fireworks.

They waited outside the cafe and Kaz went to the shop to get his bike. Then they walked along Radford Street.

'Nice bike,' Luca said to Kaz.

'Yeah, thanks …' Kaz said.

15 'Did you buy it here in Plymouth? Which shop did you buy it in?' Luca asked.

'Er … I bought it in … er … London,' Kaz answered.

'I'd love a bike like that,' Luca said. Then he saw a small sticker on the bike. It said:

20 COGS-BIKES, Drake Circus, Plymouth

'That's strange,' Luca thought. But he said nothing.

The kids walked past the Hoe. There were lots of people on the grass. Then they walked past the Lido. It was a warm day, so that was busy too. At last they came to *Captain* 25 *Jaspers?* – a nice little snack place in the harbour.

'Do you know *Captain Jaspers?*' Mia asked Kaz.

'No, I'm new in Plymouth,' he answered.

'It's the best place. The ice cream is great,' Ellie said.

The five kids got ice cream and sat at a table.

'When did you come to Plymouth?' Luca asked Kaz.

'Last month,' Kaz answered.

'Where do you live in Plymouth?' Adam asked.

'Er … where the ships are …' Kaz answered.

'Oh, near the harbour? That's nice,' Mia said.

'Do you like it here?' Ellie asked.

'Yes, it's very nice,' Kaz answered and he smiled at Ellie.

'Do you miss London?' Mia asked.

'No, this is my home now. I'm not going back to London,' Kaz said, but he didn't smile. He looked down.

'It's the Summer Festival fireworks this evening. Where can we watch?' Adam asked.

'Let's go to the Hoe. You can see everything there,' Luca said.

'Good idea,' Ellie said. 'Do you want to come too, Kaz?'

'Sure. Great, thanks,' Kaz said. He looked happy.

'Maybe Luca is right,' Adam thought. 'Maybe I'm too suspicious. Maybe Kaz is really OK. The others like him.'

The kids ate their ice cream, walked to the Hoe, and sat to watch the fireworks. Ellie only had a T-shirt and she was a bit cold.

'Do you want to borrow my jacket?' Kaz said.

He gave Ellie the blue jacket. She was very happy.

'What school are you at here in Plymouth? Are you at our school – Eggy?' Mia asked Kaz.

'Er … no … I'm at a different school … it's Plym …'

'Is it Plymstock School?' Ellie asked.

'Yes,' Kaz said. 'I started last month.'

'Cool,' Luca said. 'My cousin goes to Plymstock School. You can meet him. He's coming to the fireworks.'

Kaz didn't answer. After a few minutes he said, 'I have to go home now. I'll see you tomorrow – at the cafe. Thanks for the ice cream.'

'But what about the fireworks?' Ellie asked. She looked
5 disappointed.

'Sorry. I have to go now … Bye.'

'And your jacket, Kaz …' Ellie shouted. But it was too late. Kaz was gone.

The four friends were surprised.
10 'That's so strange,' Adam thought. 'I really don't understand Kaz. He's hiding something.'

CHAPTER 5 **Kaz alone**

What happened in the last chapter? Kaz went with the four friends to Captain Jasper's. They had a nice time. But then Kaz left suddenly. The four friends didn't understand that.

Ellie, Mia, Luca and Adam were very nice. Kaz liked them. But they asked too many questions and Kaz didn't like the questions. And he didn't want to meet Luca's cousin because he didn't want to talk about Plymstock School. So he left the four friends on the Hoe. He walked away quickly and he pushed his bike.

When he got to the flat, he stopped at the big gate. He pressed buttons and put in the code. The gate opened and Kaz pushed the bike into the garden. He locked it carefully. There were some kids in the street. He looked at them. He was surprised – it was Adam, Mia, Ellie and Luca.

'Have they seen me?' he asked himself. He didn't want to meet them here. He opened the door of the flat quickly and went inside. The flat was empty and quiet. There was nobody there.

Kaz sat down at the table. He took a tin of beans out of his bag and opened it. He got a spoon from the kitchen and he ate the beans from the tin. He took some bread out of his bag and he ate that too. He had no butter for the bread. Then he carefully put the empty tin back in his bag. He washed the spoon and put it back in the kitchen.

Kaz took a photo out of his bag and he looked at it. It was an old photo of a man in a sailor's uniform. The man was on the Hoe in Plymouth.

The man in the photo looked like Kaz. Kaz looked at the back of the photo and read the words again: *Dear Henry, I miss you. I'll come back to get you soon. Love, Dad*
Kaz felt sad and lonely.

5 'Where are you now, Dad?' he thought. He didn't know. Was his dad still in Plymouth? Maybe. Was he on one of the boats? Maybe.

'I don't know where you are, Dad. But if you're here, I'll find you,' Kaz thought.

Suddenly the doorbell rang. Kaz jumped. Who was that? He never had visitors in the flat. Nobody knew that he lived here. Kaz went to the window carefully and he looked into the street. He could see four people at the gate.
5 Oh no! It was the four friends. So they saw him in the garden! They knew he lived here. That was terrible. What should he do? Should he go to the door?

Kaz just waited. The doorbell rang … and rang … and rang.

What happened in the last chapter? Kaz went back to his flat. He ate alone. The four friends rang his doorbell. But Kaz didn't want to see them. He didn't go to the door.

5 Kaz was gone. The four friends were on the Hoe. They wanted to find a better place to watch the fireworks, but it was full. The kids walked around but there were too many people.

10 'Let's go to the harbour, near the Lido,' Mia said.

'Yes, that's a good idea. Maybe there's more space there,' Luca said.

So they walked down the hill and they went along some small streets to the harbour. When they were on Hoe 15 Road, Adam stopped suddenly.

'Look over there,' he said. 'Do you see the boy with the bike?'

The others looked but it was difficult to see.

'Yes, that's Kaz,' Ellie said. She was surprised. They 20 were all surprised.

'But Kaz said that he lived in Stoke. This isn't Stoke,' Adam said.

'Oh Adam. You're always suspicious. Maybe he's visiting friends,' Mia said.

25 'But he's new here. I don't think that he has friends in Plymouth,' Luca said.

The friends watched the boy. He locked his bike and went into one of the flats. They were beautiful flats – very big, very modern, very expensive. They had big windows with a view of the sea.

5 'I know!' Ellie said. 'Kaz is a rich kid. Look at the flats. Look at his bike. Look at this designer jacket. He's a rich kid and he's embarrassed about it. He doesn't want us to know!'

'I don't know,' Adam said. 'This is very strange.'

10 Adam really was suspicious.

'Hey guys, I have an idea. This would be a great place to watch the fireworks,' Ellie said.

'Yeah, let's ring Kaz's doorbell. We'll give him a big surprise,' Mia said.

15 'Great idea,' Luca said. 'Rich friends are cool! Maybe Kaz has some nice food for us!'

'I don't know about this,' Adam said. 'I don't think Kaz wants to see us …'

The kids talked for a few minutes. Ellie and the others
20 really wanted to visit Kaz. But Adam still wasn't sure. In the end Ellie went to the gate and she looked at the name on the doorbell.

'Hey Adam, what's Kaz's name? Kaz what?' Ellie asked.

'His real name is Henry Kazwell,' Adam answered.

25 'Kazwell?' Ellie said. 'The name here is "Coleman", not Kazwell. But maybe his mum or his dad has a different name. Let's ring the doorbell and we'll see,' Ellie said.

'No! ' Adam said. But Ellie rang the doorbell on the gate. There was no answer. She pushed again and again.
30 Nothing happened. Kaz didn't come out.

'Adam, do you have Kaz's mobile number?' Luca asked.

'No, I don't,' Adam said. 'Mum asked him for his number, but he doesn't have a mobile.'

'That's strange – a rich kid without a mobile,' Luca said.

'Oh Luca, you're suspicious too. Maybe Kaz's parents
5 think mobiles are unhealthy,' Ellie said.

'Maybe we don't know Kaz's real story!' Adam said suspiciously.

The four kids walked slowly away from the flat. They stopped for a minute and looked back. Adam thought he
10 saw a face in a window, but he wasn't sure. Why didn't Kaz open the door? Who was Henry Kazwell really?

The others laughed and chatted. They walked to the harbour and forgot about Kaz.

'Whiiiiiizzzz bang!' There was a loud noise and lots of
15 colour over Plymouth.

'The fireworks are starting!,' Luca shouted.

What happened in the last chapter? The four friends saw Kaz at the flat. But he didn't open the door.

 The fireworks over Plymouth were amazing. Kaz sat alone at the window of the big flat and
5 he watched. He thought about the four friends.

'They're having a nice time together,' he thought. 'Everything is OK for them. They have normal families, normal homes. But for me it's different …'

He was tired after his busy day and it was late. So Kaz
10 went to bed on the sofa in the living room. He thought about tomorrow. He planned to go to the harbour after work – like he did every evening. He liked to watch the big ships and the sailors. Maybe he'd see his dad … maybe … maybe … He went to sleep.

15 Later that night: Suddenly there was noise in the flat … noise in the hall … voices … Somebody was in the flat! Kaz jumped up quickly, picked up his shoes and bag, and went quietly into the kitchen. Then he heard voices in the sitting room … a man … a woman … a boy …

20 'It's good to be home again,' the man said.

'I'm tired, Dad. I'm going to bed. Good night,' the boy said.

'Night, darling,' the woman said. 'I'd like a cup of tea before I go to bed.'

25 'Me too,' the man said. 'I'll make it.'

Kaz quickly opened the back door and went into the garden. The man came into the kitchen.

'It's cold in here,' he said and went to the door.

'Oh look,' the man said. 'The back door is open!'

'What?' the woman said. 'Did we really leave the door open when we were in Spain?'

5 'Or was someone in our flat?' the man asked.

Kaz hid behind a tree in the garden. He was very scared. The man and the woman looked into the garden, but they saw nothing.

'Everything is normal here,' the woman said.

'Oh dear, oh dear! I think we left the back door open for a week! How stupid!' the man said.

Kaz waited until everybody was in bed. Then he tried to climb the wall of the garden, but it was too high. So he
5 went to the garage and got some boxes. He put the boxes beside the wall, very carefully and very quietly. Then he climbed up and jumped …
  Thump! Kaz fell on the road. He got up slowly. His leg hurt, but he could walk. Then he went along Hoe Road
10 quietly.

When Kaz came to the harbour, he stopped. His leg still hurt and he was still frightened. He was surprised the people were home so soon.
  'Maybe the people will see that I was there,' he thought.
15 But he was always very careful. The flat was clean and the bike was in the garden. All his things were in his bag and he had that with him. So he should be OK.
  And then he suddenly remembered the jacket, the blue designer jacket. It wasn't his jacket. It was from the flat.
20 And now Ellie had it.
  'Oh no!' he thought. 'They'll miss the jacket.'
  It was very late. There were no people in the street, just one or two cars. Then he saw some blue lights – a police car. Maybe the people in the flat called the police. He hid.
25 And he thought,
  'What am I going to do now? I can't stay here. But where can I go? Where can I sleep?'
  His leg hurt. He was tired and he was lonely. And now maybe he was in trouble with the police.
30 'What should I do now?' Kaz asked himself.

25

CHAPTER 8 **The mystery of the jacket**

What happened in the last chapter? The owners of the flat came back and Kaz had to leave. But he had no place to go, no place to sleep.

 The next morning the cafe was quiet. Adam sat
5 beside the window and cut some vegetables for the soup of the day. He didn't like this job – it was boring. So he watched the road and waited for Kaz because had some questions for him.

Then Adam saw Tom. The old man brought some big boxes
10 from his car into the shop – alone. Where was Kaz? Why wasn't he with Tom? Adam walked to Tom's shop.

'Hello, Tom. How are you this morning?' Adam asked.

Tom didn't look very happy. He looked tired too.

'Not so good, Adam,' he said. 'Kaz isn't here yet and I
15 need help. Do you know where he is?'

'No. We saw him last night. We went to *Captain Jaspers* together. But then he went home,' Adam answered.

'I have another problem,' Tom said.

'What's the problem?' Adam asked.

20 'Come into my shop and I'll show you,' Tom said.

He and Adam went into the shop. They went to a table near the door.

'Do you see the things on this table? They're all things that are a bit old. Their sell-by date is today or tomorrow.
25 So they're special offers,' Tom said.

'Yes,' Adam said. 'I often buy things from this table –
like biscuits or cakes. They're good value. But I don't
understand. What's the problem?'

'Well, some things are missing from this table. It isn't a
5 big problem because the things are cheap. But I'm a bit
worried …' The old man looked a little sad.

'Er … Do you think it's Kaz?' Adam asked carefully.

'No! Kaz is a good boy. I like him … I don't think …'
The old man didn't want to think anything bad about Kaz.

10 Later, when Adam was back in the cafe, he told his mum
about Tom and Kaz.

'Kaz is a nice boy,' his mum said. 'Maybe he's ill.'

'Yes,' Adam thought. 'Maybe he's ill. Maybe that's why
he went home quickly last night. Maybe that's why he
15 didn't come to the door. Oh I'm too suspicious.'

Adam sent a text to his friends:

*'Come to the cafe. Kaz is missing. Maybe he's ill. You have to
help me.'*

Adam, Ellie, Luca and Mia decided to go to Kaz's flat again.
20 They rang the doorbell and this time a man opened the
door. Maybe it was Kaz's father.

'Hello,' the man said. He was friendly.

'Hi,' Ellie answered. 'We'd like to talk to Kaz, please.'

'Who?' the man asked. He looked surprised. 'There's no
25 Kaz here.'

Luca saw the red bike in the garden.

'But that's his bike,' Luca said.

'That's Andrew's bike – my son,' the man said.

Then a boy – about 15 – came to the door. He looked at
30 the four friends. He looked at Ellie.

He said, 'That's like my jacket. I can't find my jacket ...'

'I borrowed this jacket from a friend,' Ellie said.

Then Ellie knew that something was very wrong. Kaz must be in trouble.

5 'This must be your jacket,' she said and she gave the jacket to the boy.

'Come on,' Ellie said to the others. 'Let's go.'

The four friends left quickly. They had to find Kaz!

The boy and his dad stood at the door, and they really 10 didn't understand.

What happened in the last chapter? Kaz didn't go to work. Old Tom had a problem in his shop. And Kaz was missing. The friends had to find him.

Kaz woke up slowly. He didn't feel very well. He looked around but at first he didn't know where he was. There were boxes everywhere. Then he remembered – he was in the yard behind the cafe.

'I have to hurry,' he thought. 'I don't want to meet Adam here, or Adam's mum. And I have to get to Tom's shop quickly.' His leg still hurt so he got up slowly.

Then he heard a noise. Suddenly the back door of the cafe opened and somebody came into the yard. It was Adam's mum.

'Who's there!' she shouted when she saw somebody between the boxes.

'Sorry, Mrs Osmanovic. It's me – Kaz. I … er …' Kaz said. He didn't know what to say. He was very embarrassed.

'Kaz! Everybody is looking for you. Are you OK?' Adam's mum said. 'Did you sleep here? Are you in trouble?' She was very worried.

'I'm OK,' Kaz said. 'But I think I have to tell you the real story.'

Ten minutes later Kaz was in the cafe at a table with a big English breakfast. Adam and his friends were back. Tom was there too. Kaz started to tell his story:

'When I was young, I lived in London with my mum and dad. But my dad left. He had no job. And he and mum … well, they had some problems. Things were difficult. So dad went to Plymouth. I was very sad. I loved my dad. He was very important for me, so I really missed him. At first he often wrote cards, letters, emails … Then he got a job on a big boat in Plymouth. He was a sailor and he went to lots of countries – Brasil, China, Australia, … But he always came back to Plymouth. Look. I have a photo of him.'

Kaz took out the old photo and showed it to everybody. At first they were all quiet.

'He looks very nice and you look just like him,' Ellie said.

'How old is the photo?' Mia asked.

'About eight years old,' Kaz said.

'And do you still get emails from him?' Luca asked.

'No, the emails and cards stopped about eight years ago,' Kaz said. 'We wrote to his boat, but he left his job. They didn't know where he was.'

'Did he stay in Plymouth?' Tom asked.

'I don't know,' Kaz answered. 'I'm looking for him now, you see?'

'And have you tried the internet?' Adam's mum asked.

'Yes, I've tried everything, but no news.' Kaz looked very sad.

'What about your mum. Can she help you?' Adam asked.

'My mum died last year. She had some problems – big problems. You know, with drugs ...' Kaz said.

'Oh that's terrible. Poor you,' Mia said.

Then Kaz spoke again:

'First I lived with a foster family in London. But it was difficult. I didn't like my foster dad. He was very strict. And I wasn't very good ... I didn't go to school ... I stayed out late ... I did stupid things ... '

'So what happened then?' Adam asked.

'When I was 16, my sister said I could live with her and her boyfriend. That was the plan. But her boyfriend didn't like me. It was clear he didn't want me around. I didn't want my sister to be in trouble, so I left London and came to Plymouth. I wanted to find my dad. I wanted to live with him. I called my sister and said I had a flat and a job in Plymouth'

'So did you find a flat in Plymouth?' Tom asked.

'No. I had no money and no job. At first the weather was good so I could sleep in the parks or by the sea. Then one day I met a boy – Andrew. We talked a lot. He told me about his holiday plans, with his family in Spain. So I followed him. I know it's terrible, but I watched him. I learned the code for his gate. And I saw where he hid the keys to the flat. So I stayed in the flat for a week – until yesterday, when the family came home.'

Kaz stopped for a minute. Everybody waited. Then Kaz spoke again:

'And Tom, I took some food from your shop. I'm sorry. I was hungry. But I know it was wrong. I'm going to pay you for the food.'

'Don't worry about the food, Kaz. It isn't important,' Tom said.

'But what are you going to do now?' Ellie asked.

'I don't know,' Kaz said. He looked down.

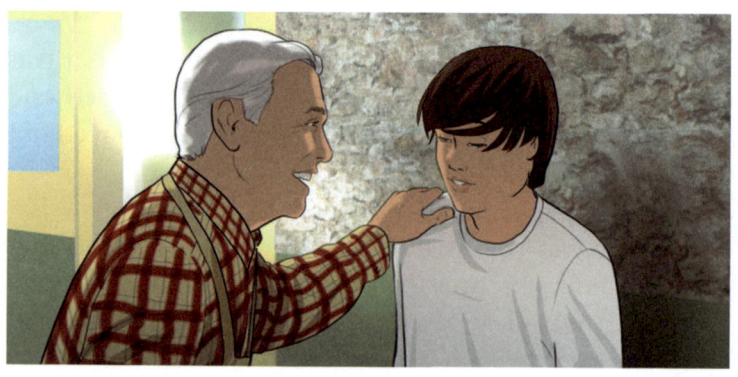

Then Tom said, 'You must learn something, Kaz. If you have problems, you have to ask for help.'

'Tom is right,' Adam's mum said. 'We can help you. I have an idea …'

CHAPTER 10 **Looking forward**

5 **What happened in the last chapter?** Kaz told his real story. He has no home, no expensive flat, no rich parents. He wants to find his dad.

That evening Kaz moved into Adam's house. Adam's mum said he could stay there for a few weeks, until he found his 10 own place.

In the next week Tom helped Kaz to look for a new place. They found out about Plymouth Newstart. It was a place for young people who have no home. Kaz and Tom went there and they spoke to a woman.

15 'How old are you,' the woman asked.

'I'm 16,' Kaz answered.

'Good,' the woman said and smiled. 'We have rooms for people from 16 to 25 years.'

'How much does a room cost?' Tom asked.

20 'It's £11 for a week. You get your own room and you share a kitchen,' she answered.

'That's great and it isn't expensive,' Kaz said. 'When can I move in?'

'Let me see,' she said and looked in her book. 'There's a free room in September.'

5 The next day Kaz was in the cafe. He was very happy and he talked about the room at Plymouth Newstart.

'What about school?' Adam's mum asked.

'Kaz is at Plymstock School,' Adam told her.

'Er, no, I'm not. That wasn't true … I'm not at any 10 school … I left my school in London,' he said. He was embarrassed.

'But Kaz, you have to think about your future. You have to go back to school,' Adam's mum said.

'What about Eggy – our school? Maybe you can go 15 there,' Adam said.

So Kaz went with Adam's mum to Eggbuckland School and they talked to the principal, Miss Borowski. She said that Kaz could start there at the end of August.

20 One evening Kaz was in the harbour with Adam, Luca, Ellie and Mia. They looked at all the big boats and the people.

'You know Kaz, you'll never find your father like this,' Ellie said. 'You need help.'

'My aunt works for the Plymouth police. I can ask her. 25 Maybe she can help us,' Luca said.

'That's a great idea. Thanks,' Kaz said.

'And I can talk to my dad,' Adam said. 'He works on a ferry. Maybe he can help us too.'

'Wow, that's fantastic,' Kaz said.

30 'And I have another idea,' Mia said. 'Let's go and talk to …'

The five friends chatted about their plans and ideas.

And so Kaz's new life in Plymouth started. He had a new home, new friends and a new future. And he had hope.

A

accent: ['æksənt] Akzent

amazing: [ə'meɪzɪŋ] erstaunlich, toll

appetite: ['æpɪtaɪt] Appetit

around: [ə'raʊnd] umher, herum

Australia: [ɒ'streɪliə] Australien

B

back door: [ˌbæk'dɔː] Hintertür, Hintereingang

beans: [biːns] Bohnen

beside: [bɪ'saɪd] neben

Blimey!: ['blaɪmi] Mensch!, Verdammt!

boat: [bəʊt] Boot, Schiff

Brazil Brasilien

button: ['bʌtn] Knopf

C

China: ['tʃaɪnə] China

code: [kəʊd] Code, Kennzahl

(to) cost: [kɒst] kosten

customer: ['kʌstəmə] Kunde

D

darling: ['dɑːlɪŋ] Liebling

decided: [dɪ'saɪdɪd] (to) decide beschließen, entscheiden (decide, decided, decided)

designer: [dɪ'zaɪnə] Designer

doorbell: ['dɔːbel] Türklingel

drugs: Drogen

F

famous: ['feɪməs] berühmt

fantastic: [fæn'tæstɪk] fantastisch, toll

floor: [flɔː] hier: Fußboden

followed: ['fɒləʊd] (to) follow folgen, verfolgen (follow, followed, followed)

foster family: ['fɒstəˌfæməli] Pflegefamilie

frightened: ['fraɪtnd] erschreckt, beängstigt

funfair: ['fʌnfeə] Jahrmarkt

G

gate: [geɪt] Tor

grandson: ['grænsʌn] Enkel(sohn)

H

high: [haɪ] hoch

himself: [hɪm'self] sich selbst

hope: [həʊp] Hoffnung

(to) hurry: ['hʌri] sich beeilen

J

jumped: [dʒʌmpt] (to) jump springen, hüpfen (jump, jumped, jumped)

K

key: [kiː] Schlüssel

L

light: [laɪt] Licht
lighthouse: ['laɪthaʊs]
    Leuchtturm
(to) lock: [lɒk] (ab)schließen
loud: [laʊd] laut

O

own: [əʊn] eigene/-r/-s

P

paid: [peɪd] (to) pay
    bezahlen (pay, paid, paid)
pressed: [prest] (to) press
    drücken, betätigen
    (press, pressed, pressed)
pushed: [pʊʃt] (to) push
    hier: schieben
    (push, pushed, pushed)

R

rang: [ræŋ] (to) ring
    klingeln, läuten
    (ring, rang rung)
rich: [rɪtʃ] reich

S

sailor: ['seɪlə] Seefahrer, Segler
ship: [ʃɪp] Schiff
son: [sʌn] Sohn
spoon: [spuːn] Löffel
sticker: ['stɪkə] Aufkleber
suspicious: [sə'spɪʃəs] to be
    suspicious
    misstrauisch sein

T

thump: [θʌmp] dumpfer Schlag
tin: [tɪn] Blechdose
traffic: ['træfɪk] Verkehr

W

washed: [wɒʃt] to wash
    waschen
    (wash, washed, washed)
waved: [weɪvd] (to) wave
    winken
    (wave, waved, waved)

Y

yard: [jɑːd] Hof

Chapter 1

1 Kaz lives in Plymouth now, but what was his home town?

2 What does Kaz think about Plymouth?

3 What does Kaz do when the boy from the cafe says ‚hello'?

4 Why is Tom happy with Kaz?

Chapter 2

1 Adam thinks the boy with the red bike is rich. Why does he think that?

2 Adam thinks the boy with the red bike is hiding something. Why does he think that?

Chapter 3

1 Where is Kaz's new afternoon job?

2 How does Kaz feel about Adam's questions?

3 What do Mia and Ellie think about Kaz?

Chapter 4

1 Why does Luca think it's strange that Kaz bought his bike in London?

2 What does Kaz do when Ellie is cold?

3 What happens at the end of the chapter? Why are the four friends surprised?

Chapter 5

1 Why did Kaz suddenly leave the four friends on the Hoe?

2 Who is the man in the photo?

3 What does Kaz do when the doorbell rings?

Chapter 6

1 Why do the four friends ring the doorbell?

2 Why don't they call Kaz on his mobile?

3 Why does Adam think that Kaz doesn't want to see the four friends?

Chapter 7

1 Who does Kaz hear in the night?

2 How does Kaz hurt his leg?

3 Why does Kaz hide when he sees blue lights?

Chapter 8

1 Why is Tom unhappy?

2 What do the four friends find out when they go back to the flat?

3 Who owns the blue jacket?

Chapter 9

1 Why is Kaz in the yard behind the cafe?

2 What does Kaz tell the others about his parents?

3 Why did Kaz come to Plymouth?

4 Where did Kaz live when he came to Plymouth?

5 Who took the food in Tom's shop?

Chapter 10

1 What is different about Kaz's new life in Plymouth?

2 Why does Kaz have hope at the end of the story?